Lighthouses
Watchers at Sea

*Here's a list of other nonfiction
Redfeather Books from Henry Holt*

*Available in paperback

Brenda Z.
Guiberson

Lighthouses

· · · · · · ·

Watchers at Sea

WITH ILLUSTRATIONS

BY THE AUTHOR

· · ·

A Redfeather Book

HENRY HOLT AND COMPANY

NEW YORK

Henry Holt and Company, Inc., *Publishers since 1866*
115 West 18th Street, New York, New York 10011

Henry Holt is a registered
trademark of Henry Holt and Company, Inc.

Published in Canada by Fitzhenry & Whiteside Ltd.,
195 Allstate Parkway, Markham, Ontario L3R 4T8.

Library of Congress Cataloging-in-Publication Data
Guiberson, Brenda Z.
Lighthouses: watchers at sea / Brenda Z. Guiberson,
with illustrations by the author.
p.   cm.—(A Redfeather Book)
Includes bibliographical references.
Summary: Recounts the history of lighthouses from the struggle
to build invincible towers, through heroic rescues of lost ships,
to the haunted tales surrounding these isolated structures.
1. Lighthouses—United States—History—Juvenile literature.
[1. Lighthouses.] I. Title. II. Series.
VK1023.G85 1995   387.1'55'0973—dc20   95-4204

ISBN 0-8050-3170-7/First Edition—1995
Printed in the United States of America
on acid-free paper.∞
1 3 5 7 9 10 8 6 4 2

Permission for use of the following photographs
is gratefully acknowledged: pages iv–v (North Head Light,
Washington State) © Ray Atkeson/American Landscapes;
page x (Westchop lighthouse, Martha's Vineyard, Massachusetts)
© Alison Shaw; page 64 (detail, Edgartown lighthouse, Martha's
Vineyard, Massachusetts) © Alison Shaw.

To my son, Jason,
as his own journey begins

Contents

Lighthouses
Watchers at Sea

Edgartown lighthouse on Martha's Vineyard, Massachusetts, stands ready to guide mariners through tempestuous storms. *Copyright Alison Shaw.*

· 1 ·

Lighthouses Tall and Bright

It is the scene of the most heart-rending disasters . . .
causing the death of many a brave seaman.

• • •

—Minots Ledge, a rocky reef near
Boston, 1840s, described by
Inspector I.W.P. Louis of Lighthouse Service

I t is August 1635, and a day when a terrible hurricane swirls across the Atlantic Ocean near Boston. The furious wind pounds the raindrops through the air and churns up huge waves that crash over a small ship caught in the storm. The ship tilts up, then sideways, then plunges downward as it tosses on the water. Everything that is not tied down washes overboard. Anthony Thatcher holds tightly to his wife and four children so they will not be swept away. Their clothing is soaked, and the children feel seasick and cold. Shivering, they huddle together and try to hold on to the ropes.

The captain shouts a command to his crew. His words are whipped away and never heard in the loud, screaming

Today, it is easier for sailors to find safe harbor in a storm. Menemsha, Massachusetts, at the height of Hurricane Bob. *Copyright Alison Shaw*.

winds. Another huge wave smashes across the deck, and the ship spins and tosses again. The captain looks into the stormy sky but cannot even see the bow of his ship. Somewhere there is a harbor, but where? In another direction are sharp, dangerous rocks, but which way? He clings to the steering wheel but does not know if he should pull it to the left or to the right.

It is too late to decide. Suddenly he hears a terrible *scritch-crunch* as the ship smashes across the grinding teeth of a rock island. In the sudden jolt Anthony Thatcher and his wife are thrown onto shore. They are the only ones to survive the shipwreck. Their four children and fifteen others die as the storm cracks the ship and then sinks it into the sea.

This terrible disaster, on a place that has come to be known as Thatcher's Island, has been repeated thousands and thousands of times for as long as people have gone out on the water. There was no lighthouse on this island in 1635. A tower was finally built in 1771, but only after many other shipwrecks. People have always known that mariners need help on a stormy sea, but it has been very difficult to find a good way to provide it. The best help for ships caught in a storm is a lighthouse with a strong light or fog signal to guide them.

The first lights built for mariners long ago were great bonfires burning along the shore. After a while people discovered that elevated fires could be seen from a greater distance than those on the beach. They began to build high stone towers and burn the fires up on top.

One of the greatest stone lighthouses was built in Alexandria, Egypt, in 280 B.C. It guided ships in the Mediterranean Sea for more than a thousand years and made the

At the Pharos in Egypt, mariners said that smoke was sometimes a better guide than fire.

harbor a very important and safe place for the shipping business. The lighthouse, called the Pharos, was considered one of the Seven Wonders of the World. The Pharos became so well known that in many different languages, some version of this word means lighthouse. In English, the study of lighthouses is called pharology.

The Pharos was as tall as a forty-story building and could be seen from a great distance. What did this mean to the mariners at sea?

Well, if a light is one hundred feet above sea level, it can be seen from a distance of about thirteen miles. If the light is as tall as the Pharos, it can be seen for almost thirty miles. Building something high above the horizon of the land helps in seeing it farther over the curve of the earth. This is why a lookout on a ship climbs way up into the crow's nest. High above the ship, he can spot an onshore light two or three miles before the crew on deck can see it. Every ship in a storm wants to find such a light, and as soon as possible. Using the light as a landmark, the captain can figure out where they are and know which way to sail.

Of course, a tall light can be spotted from a great distance only when the weather is clear. When the sky is full of rain, snow, or fog, just when mariners need it the most, the light may be very dim or even impossible to see. Because of this, people have experimented, trying to come up with a more powerful light. They've also added warning sounds, such as foghorns, bells, whistles, gongs, cannons, trumpets, and even loud shouting from the shoreline, to try to help those in danger at sea.

The power of light in a lighthouse is measured in candle-power. One candlepower is the amount of light coming from a single candle. In the early history of lighthouses, when most light came from wood or coal fires, the candle-power was very low and much of the light was wasted. Some of the light blazed up into the air, some shined on the people who tended it, but most of the rays did not reach the mariners at sea.

Sometimes whale oil, kerosene, or other oils were used for fuel and burned in pans or lanterns with wicks. At other times candles were the source of light, usually many of them burning together. Candles were the easiest to take care of, but didn't burn as brightly as other fuels.

A big change in the amount of candlepower provided by a lighthouse occurred in 1781. Aimé Argand, a Swiss physicist, developed a hollow wick that allowed plenty of air to flow in and around the flame. This additional oxygen was extra food for the fire, creating a much brighter flame, with each wick now equal to seven candlepower. About the same time, lamps were also fitted with shiny metal reflectors. These curved bowls were placed behind the lights to bend the rays and direct more of them out toward the mariners. With many of these improved lamps burning together, the strength of the lantern rose to over a thousand candlepower.

Coal grate
1700s

Parabolic
reflector, 1777

Ways to Light Up
a Lighthouse

Candelabrum
Smeaton's
Eddystone, 1800

Argand lamp, 1781

Fresnel lens
first order,
the largest, 1822

Four-wick oil lamp, 1800s

Brass frame

Lamp

Glass

Reflective prism

Augustin-Jean Fresnel,
the inventor of
the Fresnel lens

Fresnel lens

Around 1815, an engineer in France who repaired high-ways began to do some exciting experiments with light and optics. His name was Augustin-Jean Fresnel (Frey-NELL). He did not have good equipment and had to use a drop of honey over a small hole cut out of cardboard to make a lens. Using the sun as his source of light, Fresnel observed how the light was distorted by the honey. Eventually he added cut-glass rings and reflecting prisms to his experiments and came up with new and more accurate ideas about the nature of light.

Fresnel used what he had learned to invent the most efficient lens ever used in lighthouses. He took all the light rays that were wasted from a flame and magnified

This Fresnel lens was awarded a gold medal at the Paris Exhibition of Industry in 1855 and then shipped to the Gay Head, Massachusetts, lighthouse. The lens is presently housed at the Vineyard Museum, Edgartown, Massachusetts. *Copyright Alison Shaw.*

them into a single powerful beam. It was a bit like taking a calm pool of water and sending it through a fire hose. From just one small light source the Fresnel lens could direct light across the water with the brightness of many thousands of units of candlepower. This incredible lens was developed in seven sizes, and many are still in lighthouses today. The intense flashing lights used on police cars and fire engines are possible because of Fresnel's ideas. In modern times his type of lens combined with a strong electric light can produce over a million candlepower.

But all this extra candlepower wouldn't help the mariners unless a solid structure could hold up the light in even the very worst storms.

Lighthouses have been built on some of the most rugged, wave-washed land in the world—places with names like Crazy Banks, the Can Opener, and Graveyard of the Pacific. Lighthouses must endure the same powerful storms and pounding waves that threaten ships. One of the most difficult and frustrating challenges in the history of lighthouses has been to figure out how to build a tower that won't become another victim of the sea.

·2·

Building an Invincible Tower

The lighthouse won't stand over tonight.
She shakes two feet each way now.

• • •

—Final message from Joseph Wilson and
Joseph Antoine, keepers at Minots Ledge, 1851

It is 1849, and the first lighthouse at Cape San Blas in Florida is finally complete. Two years later a great storm swirls around the tower and knocks it into the sea. The tower is rebuilt, but in a few months another storm pushes and lashes at it until it is destroyed again. A third lighthouse is built, but this one is seriously damaged in the Civil War. Repairs are made, but in 1869 there is a new problem: The beach begins to wash away. By 1881 the base of the tower is under eight feet of water. The next year the tower tilts, cracks, and falls into the sea. A fourth tower is built far away from the shoreline. But over the next seven years the cape continues to wash away until the new tower stands in water.

The Heceta Head lighthouse stands guard on the rugged central coast of Oregon. *Copyright Rick Schafer / American Landscapes.*

Then in another storm the lantern is damaged and the keepers' house destroyed. Finally in 1919 the lighthouse is moved a quarter mile north, where at last report it still stands today.

This is the type of story told about the building of many different lighthouses. Where one lighthouse might tilt and slip into the sea even before it is completed, others have waited until a storm gave them an extra push. The lighthouse at Brant Point in Massachusetts has been rebuilt seven times after a series of disasters with fire, storm, and rotten wood.

The very first lighthouses were built in places where it was easy to haul in supplies. The land was at the edges of harbors and usually flat and stable. But many ships ran into trouble on rocks and reefs miles offshore. For hundreds of years, no one thought lighthouses could be built in these hard-to-reach places. It took a great deal of money, daring, and experimentation to finally try. It was also necessary to ignore all the people who thought an attempt to build these lighthouses was foolish because they had never seen it done before.

The first brave effort to build offshore was made on the tiny island of Cordouan, five miles off the main coast of France. Mariners had always been terrified of the strong whirlpools swirling around this island. In 1595 the French decided to build a real lighthouse there, a great structure

The first lighthouse on Smith Island, Washington, falls apart as the island erodes. *Courtesy Coast Guard Museum Northwest, Seattle, Washington.*

A wall of timbers was built to stabilize the island under the Cordouan Island lighthouse in France.

that everyone would notice and admire. This was an amazing idea at the time, almost as if someone had suggested sending their king to the moon.

It took six boats to carry all the workers back and forth to this remote island. Soon after the work started, the island began to disappear. Quickly they built a thick wall to try to hold everything in place. This idea worked, and the construction continued. It turned out to be very, very difficult. A project that was to take two years ended up taking twenty-seven. In the end they created a fancy lighthouse, as tall as a sixteen-story building, with statues, pillars, and even a room for the king. In 1612 it was struck by lightning, which knocked twenty-five feet off the top. All the fancy designs were destroyed by the wind and the water. But the tower itself actually stood to warn mariners for hundreds of years. It changed people's thinking: Indeed, it was possible to build a good lighthouse in the middle of the sea.

Builders decided to try it again in England in 1695. This time they chose the Eddystone Reef, where two currents and tides whirl around long, jagged rocks. Sailors coming into the harbor at Plymouth always called it the "dreaded eddy stone." It was a terrifying place to travel even in daylight, when the rest of the channel was calm.

It took creativity and daring to get this project going. Only one man was willing to tackle it—a mechanical genius, joker, painter, and magician named Harry Winstanley. He loved excitement and new challenges. Already he had built a house full of inventions like trapdoors and a tricky chair that snapped its arms around anyone who sat in it. People paid to see his unusual creations, and he was both famous and rich. Unfortunately he invested his wealth in five ships and lost two of them on the Eddystone.

He did not have an easy task building a lighthouse on the Eddystone rocks. The only place to build the tower was on a slippery, slanted rock about as wide as a house. The work was limited to the best days of summer. Winstanley and his crew spent most of the time rowing the fourteen miles back and forth to the reef. Once, they were attacked by French privateers and Winstanley was imprisoned in France. But when the French king recognized his prisoner, he released him quickly. "Your work," he told Winstanley, "is for the benefit of men of all nations using the seas."

The next year the crew finally decided to try an overnight stay on the Eddystone. A huge storm came up, and according to Winstanley, "It was eleven days before any boat could come near us again." They spent the whole time "neer[*sic*] drowned with wet and all our provisions in as bad a condition."

Later the tower had to be redesigned and built taller because the lantern was getting soaked by the bigger waves that washed over the Eddystone. Eventually the lighthouse was completed and the candles were lit. It was a stunning achievement, and people all along the coastline rowed out in boats or flocked to the beaches and cliff tops just to see it.

The Eddystone Lights

Henry Winstanley
1644–1703

Rudyerd's tower
in flames

Winstanley's
tower—
rebuilt, 1699;
Lost in storm

Winstanley's tower,
1698; Too low

Rudyerd's tower,
1709—Wood
burned in fire

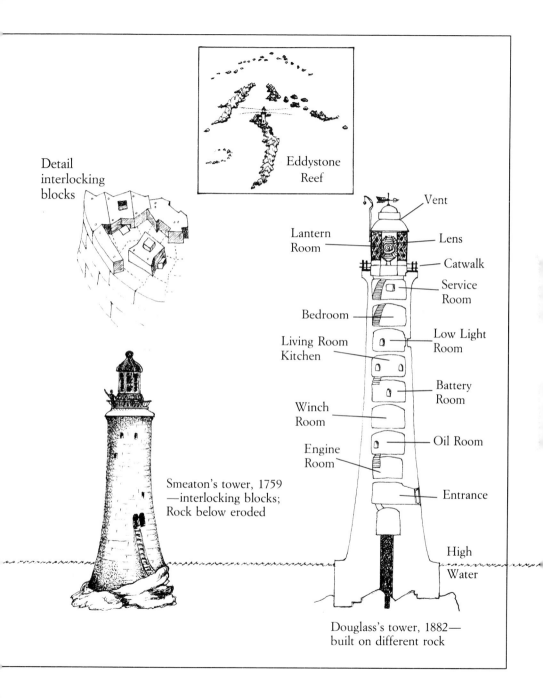

Detail interlocking blocks

Eddystone Reef

Vent

Lantern Room

Lens

Catwalk

Service Room

Bedroom

Low Light Room

Living Room Kitchen

Battery Room

Winch Room

Oil Room

Engine Room

Entrance

Smeaton's tower, 1759
—interlocking blocks;
Rock below eroded

High Water

Douglass's tower, 1882—
built on different rock

For five years the light on the Eddystone safely protected the mariners. Then a great storm blew through the area. When it was over, Winstanley headed right out to inspect the lighthouse. Unfortunately for him, the storm still had one final blast that became the worst screaming wind ever to hit England. It shredded houses, drove roof tiles eight inches into the ground, and drowned thousands of sheep. On the water, one hundred fifty ships were wrecked and eight thousand sailors lost at sea. Winstanley, who always said that he wanted to be in his lighthouse "during the greatest storm that ever was," got his wish. He and the tower disappeared that night and were never seen again.

Just two days later another ship was wrecked on the Eddystone. It was the first disaster since the lighthouse had been built. There was little doubt in anyone's mind now that they needed to try again.

The man to build the second Eddystone light was a silk merchant named John Rudyerd. He asked shipbuilders to help him with the design. Timbers were used for much of the structure and carefully fitted together and waterproofed with pitch, just like a ship. It turned out to be a good design. The early reports were so encouraging that people stopped climbing up the cliffs after every storm just to see if it was still standing. But timber was the wrong material. After about twenty-five years shipworms began to chew up the wood. Then in 1755 the candles in the lantern started a fire and the entire structure burned down.

So they tried again. The third lighthouse was designed by John Smeaton, an engineer. He made ten trips out to study the reef but was able to reach it only four times because of the terrible weather. He decided to cut stones on land and transport them out to the site. He came up with such a good way to fit the stones together that his tower outlasted the rock underneath, which eroded away after another one hundred twenty-five years. Smeaton's lighthouse served as a good model for many rock towers to follow, including the fourth Eddystone light, which is still in use today.

But lighthouses eventually were built for other situations—some on squishy mud or shifting sand, others that would be battered all winter by huge chunks of ice. Not every lighthouse would be built with fitted stones like those on Smeaton's tower.

The first lighthouse built far out at sea in the United States was designed as a pile tower. It had iron legs sixty feet long and was put up in 1850 at Minots Ledge near Boston. A platform was added high above the waterline for the keepers and the lantern.

The first keeper did not like the look or feel of this long, spindly tower and quit after a big storm. In 1851 a visitor

Boulogne tower,
medieval
Ninety-six doors

Swape or
lever light,
1625; Coal basket

Isle of May,
1636; Coal beacon

Roman tower,
Dover Castle,
Medieval

during another storm wrote, "The lighthouse shakes at least two feet each way. I feel as seasick as ever I did onboard a ship." Before the tower could be reinforced, two keepers and the lighthouse disappeared into a stormy sea. Since then, better pile towers have been built, and some have done very well during hurricanes. The open spaces offer much less resistance to the wind and the waves.

In places where the ocean bottom is thick and muddy, some lighthouses have been built over huge steel drums filled with tons of concrete. An underwater chamber called a caisson is used to dig out the mud to make a good foundation. These lighthouses are called caisson lights.

In some places where it seemed impossible to erect a lighthouse of any kind, a special boat was anchored with a light to warn away the mariners. These lightships had just as much trouble in great storms as did other ships. In 1899 a lightship on the Columbia River was in "a tremen-

Fowey Rocks,
Florida, 1878—
Pile-reef light

Sandy Point,
Maryland, 1883—
Caisson light

Tillamook,
Oregon, 1881—
Rock tower

Lighthouses Old and New

Cape Hatteras,
North Carolina, 1870—
Brick tower

Brant Point,
Massachusetts, 1901—
Wood tower

Alcatraz Island,
California, 1854—
Cape Cod style

Mukilteo,
Washington, 1906—
Frame house

La Pointe,
Wisconsin, 1897—
Steel skeleton

Charleston,
South Carolina, 1962—
Elevator

Ambrose Channel,
New York, 1967—
"Texas Towers" style

Douglass's Eddystone,
1982—Helipad added

LEFT: The first Minots Ledge tower falls into the sea in 1851, near Boston, Massachusetts.

RIGHT: The second Minots Ledge tower withstands a storm. *Courtesy Coast Guard Museum Northwest, Seattle, Washington.*

dous sea, with frightful breakers." The two-inch metal anchor chains snapped and the ship was blown out of position. Immediately the keepers put out the light so they would not mislead other boats. As the storm continued, the keepers had to be rescued by a lifesaving crew that used a "breeches buoy" to pull them off the tossing ship. A breeches buoy is a pair of short pants attached to a round life preserver on a cable. It travels along a tightrope set up between the ship's mast and a sand anchor on the beach. Victims climb into the breeches buoy and rescuers on shore pull them safely over the water.

As more and more lighthouses were gradually built along the coasts, mariners could not always tell one from another. This in itself could lead to a shipwreck if the captain followed the wrong light. A system was developed where each light had its own flashing signal, every foghorn had

The *Lightship 50* grounded after a heavy storm at the mouth of the Columbia River in 1899. *Courtesy Coast Guard Museum Northwest, Seattle, Washington.*

a distinctive blast, and each paint job—solid, striped, or checkered—was different from the next. Mariners carried a chart called the Light List to check on the unique identity of each light.

The people who took care of all these lighthouses were called keepers. They spent many hours tending the lantern, all night long and through every crashing, dashing storm. It was dangerous and fascinating work, living alone so close to the beauty and power of the sea.

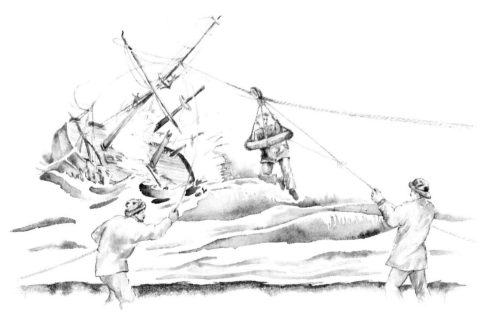

In a breeches buoy rescue, the passengers often get dunked into the sea as the ship rolls and lurches in the water.

·3·

Keepers at the Edge of the Sea

I've seen storms at Cape Saint Elias that I don't
think any ships could go through. I've seen
kelp from the beach blown right up onto the light.

• • •

—Keeper Ted Peterson, Kayak Island, Alaska

I t is 1718, and the first lighthouse in America has been in use for two years. Everyone is very proud of the Boston light because it has made the harbor safer for traveling ships. But always the sea can do things that are powerful and unexpected. On a cold November day the first keeper, George Worthylake, is rowing out to the lighthouse island with his wife, his daughter, and a friend. Their slave, Shadwell, rows out from the island to meet them. In one frightening moment a huge swell of water churns them up and tips them over. Everyone drowns.

At the time, Benjamin Franklin is a thirteen-year-old boy living in Boston. He works for a printer and writes a

A keeper and his family row out to the first Boston light.

ballad called "Lighthouse Tragedy" to sell on the streets. As the citizens buy up sheets of music for a penny, they are shocked to hear such a tragic story about their lighthouse.

Men, women, and children have all been lighthouse keepers. Many times a very difficult part of the job was making the trip out to the tower. A keeper's boat at Saddleback Ledge in Maine was also overturned by a huge wave as he rowed to his rocky station. He wrote that he "was heavily dressed at the time with long hip boots, oil pants, overalls, three shirts, and a heavy sweater. I had no chance to swim with that outfit about my body and legs." Fortunately for this keeper, a lobsterman showed up to haul him out of the water.

In 1839 at Plum Island in Massachusetts, the keeper and his wife left for a day of shopping. A sudden storm came up and they were unable to return in their small boat to light the lamp. On that dark night, without the lighthouse shining over the water, two ships hit the sandbar and many sailors drowned.

One of the hardest lighthouses to reach was Tillamook Rock in Oregon. It was often pounded by waves that could be more than a hundred feet high. Both the keepers and their supplies had to be hoisted up like a hooked fish to get onto the rock. A derrick with a cargo net or breeches buoy lifted them seventy-five feet up to a concrete landing.

Kate Walker, a keeper from 1894 to 1919 at Robbins Reef, New York, could only get into this tower by grabbing a slippery ladder from her boat and then climbing up to the kitchen. Once when she was outside in heavy sleet and snow she had to crawl on her hands and knees to get in the door.

But like all keepers, she lived at the lighthouse and rarely left it. She worked every day of the week and had many duties to perform. In the daytime, when she was not rowing her two children back and forth to school, she kept everything at the tower neat and in good repair. At sunset she lit up the lantern, and every few hours during the night she carried more fuel to the top to keep the light going.

Kate Walker had to climb a wet and slippery ladder to get into the Robbins Reef, New York, lighthouse.

She used scissors to trim and replace the wicks, and after that cleaned relentlessly. Anything that would darken the lens and windows and make the light hard to see had to be washed off. She scrubbed soot from the glass chimneys and reflectors, polished the brass, and washed smudges from the windows. Sometimes migrating birds were attracted to the light and smashed into the glass, making an extra mess to clean up. In winter, frost and snow had to be scraped from the windows. Kate was only four feet ten inches tall, and when she went outside on the narrow balcony to work, she held tightly to the handrail to keep the wind from blowing her away.

Another important part of Kate's job was winding and cleaning the clockworks that turned the lens in a circle. If this did not work properly, the light would not rotate to

A keeper cleaning a Fresnel lens. *Courtesy Coast Guard Museum Northwest, Seattle, Washington.*

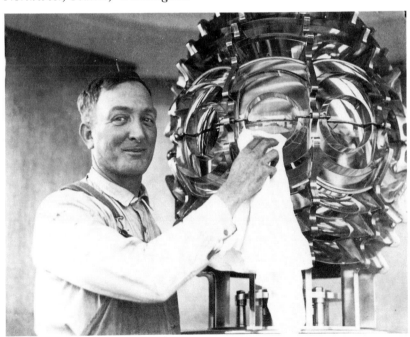

flash its special pattern. When it was too foggy for the warning light to be seen, she went down to the engine room in the cellar to start up the foghorn. It blasted every three seconds, and on foggy nights she and her children did not sleep. If the horn didn't work, then she climbed up to the top to ring the fog bell constantly, until the sky was clear again. She also kept a log and every day wrote in it the details of her job. Over the years, she recorded the times when she lowered the rowboat and went out to rescue people from the stormy sea.

Like other keepers, Kate Walker worked all night. Sometimes her son assisted. At dawn she made a final trip to the top to turn out the kerosene lights. Then she covered the lantern windows with cloth so that the powerful Fresnel lens would not magnify the light rays from the sun and start a fire in the lighthouse.

Some lighthouses had assistants, but others did not. Many keepers depended on members of their families to help out. In the early years keepers were not well paid and had no pension that would allow them to retire. They were required to be able to read, but there were many times when a keeper could hardly survive without knowing how to fix anything that broke, how to stretch a bag of flour into food for a week, or how to row a boat in twelve-foot waves and icy winds.

Many exposed lighthouses, like St. George Reef, California, often withstand waves reaching as high as the tower itself.

Keepers had to contend with unusual weather at the edge of the sea. A lighthouse and five keepers in Alaska were smashed by a tidal wave that rose up after an earthquake. A keeper at Tillamook, Oregon, wrote, "In one storm a rock weighing about 135 pounds crashed through the roof of the dwelling and demolished the kitchen range in the quarters below. On three occasions rocks have been hurled through the lantern, permitting the sea to enter and extinguishing the light." A keeper at Cape Lookout, North Carolina, spent a lot of time shoveling drifting sand away from his door. About this endless job he wrote, "The sand banks are now higher than the tops of the windows." Another keeper had to cross a dangerous and slippery walkway to reach the lighthouse and described it like this: "A terrible hurricane to-night [*sic*] at about the time of lighting up the beacon. Narrowly escaped being swept into the lake."

Keepers were often alone for weeks at a time. Some did not mind and spent the time reading or fishing. One keeper, Robert W. Tunk, at Five Finger Light Station on Frederick Sound, Alaska, watched sixteen different families of bald eagles grow up. A teenage boy, Frank Joe Raymond, took the job in Stonington, Connecticut, and over the years became a saxophone player, painter, and photographer. Laura Hecox at Santa Cruz, California, collected fossils, Indian artifacts, shells, bird eggs, and specimens from the sea. She was famous for her collection, which eventually took up an entire room in the lighthouse. But keeper Larry Marchant at Stingray Point, Virginia, wrote, "The most lonesome time that I experienced was during the winter of 1912, when I was alone for 30 days in a freeze. The tower shook while the ice was drifting

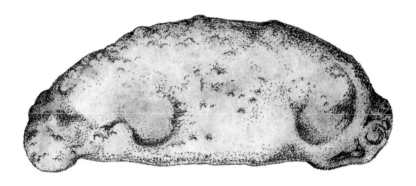

The actual size of lead chunk found in Henry Hall's stomach.

around the station and the Chesapeake was covered with ice as far as the eye could see. No kinds of boats were passing and there was nothing to look at but fields of ice."

There were keepers of every age. Henry Hall, a worker at the second Eddystone light, was ninety-four years old. He died because he actually swallowed a piece of the lighthouse when it burned down. During a fire the lantern exploded and a blob of molten lead went down Henry's throat. No one believed his story when he was rescued, but after he died, a doctor found the large chunk of metal in his stomach.

Keepers were always thinking of ways to keep a good

supply of what they needed for their job. In San Diego, California, at the old Point Loma light, the keepers made a deal with the whaling ships. They watched for whales from their high tower and the crews in return supplied them with the whale oil used for lantern fuel.

Food was a constant concern on remote sites because in bad weather the supply ship could not reach the keepers for weeks. During a long storm in New Hampshire a keeper at Boon Island was getting so desperate for food that he tossed four messages corked in bottles out to sea. A passing ship managed to read one of the messages but could not get close to the island. Instead the crew floated a barrel of food over to the lighthouse on a huge wave.

Several years later, keepers at the same lighthouse were again stranded by a storm. By Thanksgiving they had very little food left. Then they heard some loud thuds and found eight ducks that had crashed into the lantern windows. Soon they were cooking up a great Thanksgiving feast of roast duck. A hungry keeper in Alaska said, "I once made a lemon pie out of brass polish, which was high in citric acid. Made a darn good pie, too."

The keeper at the Mantinicus light in Maine left his light station and twice was unable to return for weeks at a time because of terrible storms. Each time, his daughter Abbie kept the light burning. She took care of the family and even sloshed through high seawater to save the hens. After a while they ate only one egg and a cup of cornmeal each day until her father could finally return with more food.

At Mount Desert Rock in Maine, the keepers had another supply problem. In the winter, great storms washed away every bit of soil from this tiny rock island. So in the spring, seafarers and lobstermen stopped by to replace this soil with new bags of earth. The keepers patted it down into the crevices and started again with a new garden for the summer.

Just about every keeper became a part of daring and dangerous rescues of people shipwrecked on a stormy night. The keepers went out in tiny boats in the very worst weather and brought desperate, frozen mariners back to the lighthouse. Sometimes they worked with rescue crews on the shore, shooting out lines to the ships to haul the survivors back to safety. They struggled in freezing weather with poor equipment and clothing but were very successful: In the years between 1911 and 1921, for instance, keepers rescued more than twelve hundred people.

In spite of the determination by so many to keep a light burning all night long and through every storm, there were moments in history when some people preferred the darkness. For several reasons they did not want a light to shine from the towers out to mariners at sea.

·4·

Moon Cussers and Pirates, Wartime and Ghosts

The Eliza of Liverpool came to shore
To feed the hungry and clothe the poor.

• • •

—Song about the shipwreck of the *Eliza*, 1744

It is 1807, and a huge sailing ship finally returns to Salem, Massachusetts, after a long trip to India. A strong northeast storm sweeps across Cape Anne and tosses the ship around. Suddenly, the lookout high on the mast sees great waves breaking ahead. No lighthouse was there to give an early warning and it was far too late to turn. The ship scrapes across the rocks and then cracks and crunches as the storm smashes it to pieces. A huge wave hurls the captain and some of the crew onto the rocks.

Without a lighthouse, a dark shoreline can be an ominous place for the sailor. Southshore, Martha's Vineyard, Massachusetts. *Copyright Alison Shaw.*

Soon the others and all the cargo are swept off the ship and sent bouncing and tossing into the turbulent sea.

As the great bales of cargo begin to pile up on the beach, the ship becomes part of a second drama. Now people who live nearby swarm into the area to collect clothing and furniture that wash ashore. They bring bags and wagons to haul it away. They are running, fighting, pushing, and shoving, anything to grab what they can. Some use knives and fists to make sure that they end up with a few valuables. To these people, the shipwreck seems like a gift delivered right to their beach, and everyone wants to collect as much as possible.

During our early history, people in the United States thought anything that washed up on a beach belonged to whomever got there first. But some people went a step beyond this and tried to cause the shipwreck. They worked only on the darkest of nights, when the moon was covered with clouds. These people were called "moon cussers" because of their dislike for the moonlight. The idea of a lighthouse was even worse. How could they cause a shipwreck if the captains could see where they were going?

The moon cussers didn't need much on a dark night except a lantern, a broom, and a "scrabble," which was a brick dropped into the toe of an old sock. From a danger-

Moon cussers at work, luring a ship to a rocky beach

ous rocky beach or sandbar, they would swing the lantern above their head on the broom handle. A ship at sea would see this dancing light and be fooled into thinking that it was swinging from the mast of a ship. Assuming that this ship was in a safe harbor, the captain at sea would head right for it. But then he would hear the great *crunch-crack* of the ship bottom hitting the rocks. Quickly the moon cussers would climb aboard, ready to swing the scrabble if anyone protested, and claim the ship and its cargo for themselves.

The business of wrecking ships goes far back in history. Every country had people who practiced this trade. Greeks and Romans took cargo from shipwrecks and sold the survivors as slaves. Pirates also thought wrecking was a good way to add to their wealth. Sir Ralph the Rover, an English pirate, removed a warning bell from a dangerous rock so more ships would crash there. This worked only until the stormy night when, without the bell to warn him away, he became a victim of the rock. At another place in England a huge cave called Wolf Rock howled whenever high winds blew into it. This loud howling was a good warning to ships in a storm. But the local people decided to fill the cave with stones to keep it quiet. They wanted shipwrecks. When it came time to build a lighthouse, they fought loudly against it, saying it would take away their "benefits from shipwrecks."

When lighthouses were scheduled to go up in the United States, the moon cussers protested, fought, sputtered, and fumed. They did not like these new ideas about sea safety and rescue. How would they make a living? Some moon cussers killed their victims, but others considered themselves good people because they rescued mariners from drowning and provided them with food and shelter. For a while moon cussers included a preacher and politicians and were accepted by the community. But gradually people began to change their minds.

In 1774 the state of Virginia passed a law to make this activity a crime punishable by death. In the 1780s the Massachusetts Humane Society began to build rescue sta-

Rescue at sea: SS *Mariposa* pulls to safety the crew of the SS *Edith* off Cape Saint Elias, Alaska. *Photos by J. E. Thwaites, Courtesy Special Collections Division, University of Washington Libraries, negative nos. 0020–2712, 0020–2710, 0020–2707.*

tions and shelters along the coast to store food, blankets, and firewood for survivors of shipwrecks. First, however, they had a long battle with the moon cussers, who did not want anyone meddling with their business on the beach. Moon cussers were still fighting a lighthouse scheduled for

Cape Cod in 1839, but by 1845 the society had eighteen lifesaving stations set up with boats and equipment needed for a rescue. During this period several lighthouses were destroyed by fires, and some thought this might be the work of the people who would rather wreck ships than save them.

Moon cussers weren't the only ones to fight against the lights. In 1855 a lighthouse in California became involved in the famous "egg war." Egg pickers used to collect bird eggs on the Farallon Islands and sell them at a great profit to San Francisco restaurants. This was big business because these islands are the only major seabird rookery along the Pacific coast. Each spring three hundred thousand gulls, murres, puffins, and other birds come to lay their eggs.

When a lighthouse crew showed up to build a tower, the egg pickers refused to let them land. They threw eggs and used guns and fists to threaten them. They were afraid the crew and the lighthouse would scare away the birds and they would no longer be able to make a living. Eventually the lighthouse was built, but "egg war" battles continued for many years between different groups of pickers, the government, and even the keepers. One keeper wrote, "I have a right to these eggs and I am vowed to try and gain it." In one conflict two egg pickers were killed. Sometimes boats loaded with eggs were hijacked on their way to San Francisco. Today it is illegal to collect such eggs, and these islands are an important wildlife refuge and a great place for scientists to study birds, sea lions, and elephant seals.

The egg war involved only one lighthouse, but hundreds and hundreds of lighthouses have been involved in real

Wildlife and lighthouse on Farallon Islands

wars. In times of fighting, everyone wants to control the lights—black them out when it would confuse the enemy, turn them on again to help their own ships sail into a harbor. Whoever controls the lights has a great effect on the success of planes, ships, and submarines trying to find a target.

During the Revolutionary War, British troops took over the Boston light. The American troops didn't want them to use this light, so they snuck in and burned all the wooden parts. This made the harbor dark and unsafe for navigation. The British brought in carpenters to repair it quickly, but George Washington sent three hundred more soldiers to destroy it again. When the British were finally driven out of the harbor, they didn't want anyone else to use this lighthouse. They stacked it with gunpowder, lit a slow-burning fuse, and blew the tower into the sea as they sailed away.

During the Civil War most lighthouses were controlled by the Union navy, so the Confederates tried to destroy as many lights as possible. They threw stones at the lanterns, hid the lenses, and burned anything they could. They managed to put out one hundred and sixty-four lights on the southern coast.

Over fourteen hundred lights all along the coast of the United States were blacked out during World War II.

Some lights were dimmed just enough so that they would not reveal the silhouette of a ship but still allow enough light to help friendly ships get into a harbor. Even the Statue of Liberty, which once served as a lighthouse, was blacked out during the war.

Perhaps because lighthouses have been involved in so many dramas, just about every tower comes with a ghost story. These stories are told in places where the wind moans and creaks through the doorway and the lantern casts strange shadows and then the sputtering flame goes out. The tales are heard where long spiral staircases are full of echoes, the salt spray feels like a wet blanket across the face, and the moon shines through the shadowy mist over the water. Many keepers thought the strange behavior of birds that flew straight into their lanterns could only be explained by a ghost story.

After the pile lighthouse at Minots Ledge fell into the sea, reports of a ghostlike figure began to come in. Joseph Antoine, a Portuguese fisherman, was one of the keepers to die when a great northeast storm blew over the tower. Whenever a similar storm whipped around the rebuilt lighthouse, sailors said they saw Antoine grasping the lower part of the lighthouse ladder. Always he cried out his warning, "Keep away, keep away!"

In Newport, Oregon, a young girl named Muriel went

The ghost of a mariner comes to visit the lighthouse kitchen.

with friends to visit an abandoned lighthouse at Yaquina Bay. She forgot her gloves and went back on her own to get them. There was a scream and blood was found on the steps. But Muriel was never seen again, except perhaps as a shadowy figure on the stairs, responsible for the strange wavering lights in the lantern and the swinging lamp on the beach with no one to hold it.

In the land that was to become Alaska, a Russian princess killed herself in a lighthouse just before her wedding. She did not want to be forced to marry someone she did not love. It seems she came back to haunt the lighthouse every six months, and the keepers knew her by the swish of her wedding gown, the clack of her jewelry, and the smell of sweetbrier roses. The princess ghost became just a memory after 1894, when the lighthouse burned down.

Today many lighthouses have become a memory. Just a few years ago, there were more than a thousand lighthouses in the United States. Now only a few hundred are still in use. Only the Boston light has a permanent keeper. Is this because we no longer need these lights? Absolutely not. We need safety at sea more than ever. But today we have new methods, invisible but much stronger, to help the mariners in their great ships that keep getting bigger and bigger.

Using modern technology, Martha's Vineyard's first lighthouse, built in 1799, is still able to serve Vineyard Sound, Gay Head, Massachusetts. *Copyright Alison Shaw*.

· 5 ·

Invisible Signals
to Unseen Ships

I think we're in serious trouble.

• • •

—Radio message from Third Mate
Gregory Cousins to Captain Hazelwood
on the Exxon *Valdez* after
hitting Bligh Reef, March 24, 1989

During the twentieth century huge changes came to lighthouses. Beginning around 1900 the lanterns were redesigned for electric bulbs. Compared with whale oil, candles, and kerosene, the flow of electricity involved very little work for the keepers. Later, radio waves, radio beacons, and other kinds of invisible signals hummed and buzzed their warnings to mariners at sea.

Today ships can figure out their position by using *loran* (long range navigation) signals beamed at them from shore points hundreds of miles away. They can also find signals from orbiting satellites to guide them. They use radar

A boat uses its depth finder signals to keep away from hidden rocks and reefs.

screens to look for hazards and depth finders to check the ocean floor. They listen to constant weather reports and radio chatter for updates on storms. In some areas the Coast Guard runs a vehicle traffic service with radar and radios to guide the flow of boats.

At first many sailors had a hard time accepting these invisible aids. The pulse of loran, for instance, was described as sounding like the buzz of an angry bee. Could it really be useful? Sailors preferred bright flashing lights and blasting foghorns. How could they trust something they couldn't see? In 1910 the government helped them along. They passed a law that said large boats could not operate without the new radio equipment and someone on board who knew how to use it.

The keepers, however, enjoyed the changes. In 1945 a keeper at Minots Ledge said, "It's different today, for we have radio and telephone connection with the mainland. We even have a canary out here. It isn't bad at all." Over the years remote control and automatic lightbulb changers were added to run the lighthouses. Computers, portable loran stations, steel robots, mois-ture-sensitive fog detectors, solar panels, electronic eyes, space-age acrylics—each of these changed and improved signals sent to mariners at sea.

As in any story of progress, when we come up with something new, it seems we must leave something else behind. Keepers were relieved of most of their duties and didn't have much to do besides painting the tower and washing the windows. Builders were replaced by helicop-ters that delivered portable light and fog units to places where a lighthouse could never stand. Gradually, to save money and maintenance, many lighthouses were closed

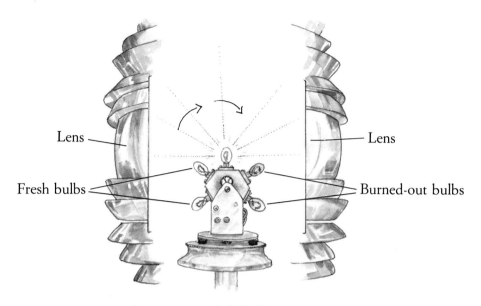

Lens — Lens

Fresh bulbs — Burned-out bulbs

An automatic lightbulb changer

and keepers removed from their watches. The lighthouses still in use run automatically with just an occasional check by the Coast Guard. The Coast Guard maintains a large rescue operation with planes, helicopters, and a fleet of boats.

Many people were concerned about the automated lighthouses. After all, an unmanned lighthouse has no one around to make rescues, no hot coffee on the stove for frozen survivors, no one to call in a personal weather report or to notice unusual conditions in the area. One Canadian fisherman said, "If you did run into trouble out there—and it's happened—the lightkeeper was always there." Many

mariners have thought of the keepers as a "security blanket" or "a friend at the light."

The keepers are no longer in the lighthouses, but ships
still look for signals to guide them. Safety at sea is more
important than ever. Today mammoth oil tankers come
into ports, along with nuclear-powered submarines, cruise
ships with thousands of passengers, and container cargoes
loaded with everything from blue jeans to chemicals to
toxic wastes. Wrecks today do not bring wealth to those
who find them. Instead, they can cause serious problems
for fish and fishermen, seabirds and beaches, the economy
and the whole ocean environment.

We now have ships as long as three football fields. The
biggest oil tankers, traveling at fifteen miles per hour, need
three miles to stop and two miles to complete a simple
turn. Even though ships can now navigate using radar,
satellites, and other signals in addition to the lighthouse,
many things can still go wrong.

Consider the story of the Exxon *Valdez*. In 1989 this
huge oil tanker was coming out of Alaska with a full load
of crude oil. The ship was being monitored by radar at a
Coast Guard station. The captain radioed for permission
to change course because he wanted to avoid icebergs in
the water. Since the radar screen revealed no other boats
in the area, permission was given. The tanker moved into

A large oil tanker, the *Arco Anchorage,* nears the Valdez Narrows, only four fifths of a mile wide, in Prince William Sound, Alaska. *Copyright Craig Fujii / Seattle Times.*

a different shipping lane but waited too long to get back. The lookout knew they were in trouble when she saw a warning light on the wrong side of the boat. But there was no longer enough room for the huge ship to turn.

The Exxon *Valdez* ended up as a shipwreck on Bligh Reef. Its bottom was ripped open as if it were a plastic bag, and eleven million gallons of crude oil poured out into the ocean. It didn't take long for the oil to coat a thousand miles of beautiful beaches and kill thousands of birds and hundreds of seals. Salmon, otters, kelp, mussels, plankton, and other life in the ocean were damaged. It was not the kind of wreck that the moon cussers or anyone else would want to claim. It was the worst oil disaster in the United States. Unfortunately dozens of other tanker wrecks around the world have been larger than this one.

Many lights still guide the mariners, but they no longer play the biggest role in preserving life at sea. Today some of the lighthouses are preserving history instead. Different groups are buying and restoring the lights that have been shut down. Some towers have become museums and parks; others are places where visitors can eat and sleep and experience a little of the life of the keepers. A few lighthouses have been kept as ideal places to watch whales and birds and the splash of the waves.

Some things about lighthouses never seem to change. Every tower continues to fight a battle with the sea and the weather. Wood, paint, metal, glass—all these materials need constant care. Lighthouses are being repainted, and having their steps rebuilt, and their lenses shined.

Vanishing shorelines, however, continue to plague even our best efforts to restore these magnificent structures. For

Wood, paint, and metal on a lighthouse gate show the effects of stormy weather by the sea. *Copyright Brenda Z. Guiberson.*

instance, many people want to save the lighthouse at Cape Hatteras off the coast of North Carolina but the land around it is washing away. Soon the tower will topple into the sea if something is not done. It will take creativity and daring, and a great amount of money, to save this lighthouse.

Why are people going to so much trouble to preserve

A volunteer paints the Edgartown lighthouse, Martha's Vineyard, Massachusetts. *Copyright Alison Shaw.*

Moving the Chappaquiddick, Massachusetts, lighthouse, one of the oldest lighthouses in the United States, back from an eroding cliff. *Copyright Alison Shaw.*

1. The top of the lighthouse is moved and placed on the ground near its present site.
2. The base of the lighthouse still in its original location. The helicopter on its way to pick up the base.
3. Base of the lighthouse being moved.
4. The top is repositioned onto the base.

these towers? One retired captain, John Olguin, in San Pedro, California, said, "I've known that lighthouse all my life." Everyone seems to like this constant, steady brightness at the edge of the sea. They like the history of the people who thought nothing was more important than involving themselves in the safety of others.

Lighthouses are the structures that hold the stories of determined keepers and builders, inventors and dreamers. A climb to the top is like taking steps with those who decided to create what was needed even though everyone said that it couldn't be done. As we look at the shiny glass lenses and old kerosene lanterns, we remember the tales of those who faced isolation and great storms and never gave up. A lighthouse is a tall, bright place to discover the beauty of the sea and the seabirds, to count the whales and smell the salt air. As the wind whispers around these great towers, it seems to say that almost anything is possible.

Bibliography

Adamson, Hans Christian. *Keepers of the Light.* New York: Greenberg Publishers, 1955.

Berenstain, Michael. *The Lighthouse Book.* New York: David McKay, 1979.

Carr, Terry. *Spill! The Story of the Exxon* Valdez. New York: Franklin Watts, 1991.

Clifford, Mary Louise, and J. Candace Clifford. *Women Who Kept the Lights: An Illustrated History of Female Lighthouse Keepers.* Williamsburg, Va.: Cypress Communications, 1993.

Cobb, Charles E., Jr. "North Carolina's Outer Banks: Awash in Change." *National Geographic,* Oct. 1987: 484–513.

Cutner, Naomi. "The Great Lighthouse Giveaway." *Life,* Aug. 1987: 36–42.

De Wire, Elinor. "Women of the Lights." *American History,* Feb. 1987: 43–48.

Giambarba, Paul. *Surfmen and Lifesavers.* Cape Cod, Mass.: Scrimshaw Press, 1985.

Gibbons, Gail. *Beacons of Light: Lighthouses.* New York: Morrow Junior Books, 1990.

———. *Sunken Treasure.* New York: HarperCollins, 1988.

Gibbs, James A. *Tillamook Light.* Portland, Ore.: Binford & Mort, 1979.

———. *Lighthouses of the Pacific.* West Chester, Pa.: Schiffer Publishing, 1986.

Holland, Francis Ross, Jr. *America's Lighthouses: An Illustrated History,* 1972. Reprint, slightly corrected, Mineola, N.Y.: Dover Publications, 1988.

Holland, F. Ross, Jr. *Great American Lighthouses.* Washington, D.C.: Preservation Press, 1989.

Knight, Frank. *Stories of Famous Ships.* Philadelphia: Westminster Press, 1966.

Lowry, Shannon. *Northern Lights: Tales of Alaska's Lighthouses and Their Keepers.* Harrisburg, Pa.: Stackpole Books, 1992.

Majdalany, Fred. *The Eddystone Light.* Boston: Houghton Mifflin, 1960.

McCabe, Carol. "Lighthouse Lore." *Early American Life,* Aug. 1991: 36–44, 78–82.

Melton, Luke. *Piloting with Electronics.* Camden, Maine: International Marine Publishing, 1987.

Nalder, Eric. "Tankers Full of Trouble," *Seattle Times,* 12–17 November 1989.

Nordhoff, Charles. *The Lighthouses of the United States in 1874.* Golden, Colo.: Outbooks, 1981.

Pilkey, Orrin. "Move It or Lose It." *Oceans,* April 1987: 23, 56.

Rand, Gloria. *Prince William.* New York: Henry Holt, 1992.

Roberts, Bruce, and Ray Jones. *Northern Lighthouses: New Brunswick to the Jersey Shore.* Chester, Conn.: Globe Pequot Press, 1990.

Schouweiler, Tom. *The Exxon-Valdez Oil Spill.* San Diego: Lucent Books, 1991.

"Shining Survivors." *Sunset,* Feb. 1986: 76–85.

Smith, Arthur. *Lighthouses.* Boston: Houghton Mifflin, 1971.

Snow, Edward Rowe. *Famous Lighthouses of America.* New York: Dodd, Mead, 1955.

———. *The Lighthouses of New England.* New York: Dodd, Mead, 1945, 1973.

———. *Pirates, Shipwrecks, and Historic Chronicles.* New York: Dodd, Mead, 1981.

Steinhart, Peter. "Island Watch." *National Wildlife,* June–July 1983: 44–50.

Stevenson, D. Alan. *The World's Lighthouses Before 1820.* London: Oxford University Press, 1959.

Swift, Hildegarde H., and Lynd Ward. *The Little Red Lighthouse and the Great Gray Bridge.* San Diego: Harcourt Brace Jovanovich, 1942, 1970.

Thurston, Harry. "The Last Lighthouse Keeper." *Canadian Geographic,* March–April 1992: 58–67.

United States Coast Guard. *Historically Famous Lighthouses.* Washington, D.C.: Government Printing Office, 1957.

Wheeler, Wayne. "Augustin Fresnel and His Magic Lantern." *The Keeper's Log,* Winter 1985: 34–38.

White, Peter. "The Farallones." *The Keeper's Log,* Fall 1988: 3–13.

Worthylake, George. "LV 50–Columbia." *The Keeper's Log,* Spring 1994: 20–23.

Index